Mind Mangler:
Member of the Tragic Circle

Henry Lewis, Jonathan Sayer and Henry Shields

T0205095

methuen | drama

LONDON • NEW YORK • OXFORD • NEW DELHI • SYDNEY

METHUEN DRAMA
Bloomsbury Publishing Plc
50 Bedford Square, London, WC1B 3DP, UK
1385 Broadway, New York, NY 10018, USA
29 Earlsfort Terrace, Dublin 2, Ireland

BLOOMSBURY, METHUEN DRAMA and the Methuen
Drama logo are trademarks of Bloomsbury Publishing Plc

First published in Great Britain 2024

Cover design by Rebecca Pitt

Cover photography by Helen Maybanks

Back cover photography by Pamela Raith

A catalogue record for this book is available from the British Library.

A catalog record for this book is available from the Library of Congress.

ISBN: PB: 978-1-3504-9643-9
ePDF: 978-1-3504-9645-3
eBook: 978-1-3504-9644-6

Series: Modern Plays

Typeset by Mark Heslington Ltd, Scarborough, North Yorkshire
Printed and bound in Great Britain

To find out more about our authors and books visit
www.bloomsbury.com and sign up for our newsletters.

Mind Mangler: Member of the Tragic Circle was first presented by Mischief on 3 August 2022 at the Pleasance Beyond Theatre as part of the Edinburgh Festival Fringe, with the following cast and creative team:

Keith/Mind Mangler	Henry Lewis
Steve/Stooge	Jonathan Sayer
Writers	Henry Lewis, Jonathan Sayer & Henry Shields
Director	Hannah Sharkey
Magic Consultant	Ben Hart
Video Designer	Gillian Tan
Lighting Designer	David Howe
Sound Designer	James Melling
Composer	Steve Brown
Production Manager	Tom Nickson
Stage Management	Jasmin Hay, Elspeth Watt, Ben Nickson & Alison Reid

The production was then presented by Kenny Wax and Stage Prescence Ltd on national UK tour in 2023, opening on 7 January 2023 at the Wyvern Theatre in Swindon with the following cast and creative team:

Mind Mangler	Henry Lewis
Steve	Jonathan Sayer
Percy/Understudy/ASM	Tom Wainwright
Writers	Henry Lewis, Jonathan Sayer & Henry Shields
Director	Hannah Sharkey
Magic Consultant	Ben Hart
Video Designer	Gillian Tan
Lighting Designer	David Howe
Sound Designer	Helen Skiera
Set Designer	Sara Perks
Costume Designer	Roberto Surace
Composer	Steve Brown
Production Manager	Tom Nickson
Company Stage Manager	Tom Platt

A one-act version of the show premiered upon the Virgin Voyages cruise ship *Resilient Lady* on 10 May 2023, with the following cast and creative team:

Mind Mangler	Killian Macardle
Steve	Jay Olpin
Writers	Henry Lewis, Jonathan Sayer & Henry Shields
Director	Hannah Sharkey
Magic Consultant	Ben Hart
Video Designer	Gillian Tan
Lighting Designer	David Howe
Sound Designer	Helen Skiera
Set Designer	Sara Perks
Costume Designer	Roberto Surace
Composer	Steve Brown
Production Manager	Tom Nickson
Consultant Stage Manager	Claire Roberts
Production Stage Manager	Naomi Slabber

The production then transferred to off-Broadway presented by Kevin McCollum, Kenny Wax & Stage Prescence Ltd, opening on 19 November 2023 at New World Stages in New York, with the following cast and creative team:

Mind Mangler	Henry Lewis
Steve	Jonathan Sayer
Percy/Understudy/ASM	Tom Wainwright & Bartley Booz
Understudy Mind Mangler	Brandon Ellis
Writers	Henry Lewis, Jonathan Sayer & Henry Shields
Director	Hannah Sharkey
Magic Consultant	Ben Hart
Video Designer	Gillian Tan
Lighting Designer	David Howe
Sound Designer	Helen Skiera
Set Designer	Sara Perks
Costume Designer	Roberto Surace
Composer	Steve Brown
Production Manager	Tom Nickson
Consultant Stage Manager	Claire Roberts
Stage Management	Adam Hunter & Christine D'Amore

The production had its West End premiere on 24 March 2024 at the Apollo Theatre in London with the following cast and creative team:

Mind Mangler	Henry Lewis
Steve	Jonathan Sayer
Percy/Understudy/ASM	Tom Wainwright
Writers	Henry Lewis, Jonathan Sayer & Henry Shields
Director	Hannah Sharkey
Magic Consultant	Ben Hart
Video Designer	Gillian Tan
Lighting Designer	David Howe
Sound Designer	Helen Skiera
Set Designer	Sara Perks
Costume Designer	Roberto Surace
Composer	Steve Brown
Production Manager	Tom Nickson
Company Stage Manager	Rachel Williams

The characters originally appeared in *Magic Goes Wrong,* co-created by Penn Jillette, Henry Lewis, Jonathan Sayer, Henry Shields and Teller. *Magic Goes Wrong* first opened on 14 December 2019 at the Vaudeville Theatre in London.

Mind Mangler:
Member of the Tragic Circle

Characters

Mind Mangler, *a mind reader*
Steve, *his stooge*
Percy, *the stage manager*

Preshow

*As the audience enter a spotlight shines on a small digital safe
downstage left. On a videotape screen (upstage centre) is an image of
the* **Mind Mangler** *and a message:*

'*CAN YOU PREDICT THE FOUR-DIGIT CODE AND OPEN
THE SAFE?*'

Mind Mangler (*voiceover*)   This is the Mind Mangler
speaking. During tonight's show I will challenge myself to
become a human lie detector. If you would like to take part
in this experiment please write a secret about yourself down
onto one of the cards provided and place it into one of the
ballot boxes. Thank you and enjoy the show.

Percy *and* **Stage Management** *collect secrets written by the
audience on cards, and place them in ballot boxes.* **Steve** *wanders
the auditorium reassuring members of the audience that no stooges
are used in the show and that if there are, he is definitely not the
stooge.*

Mind Mangler (*voiceover*)   Thank you for your secrets. They
will now be poured into these two glass bowls, which will
remain in full view throughout the performance. Please take
your seats, the show will begin shortly.

*The collected secrets are poured into two glass bowls that sit stage left
and stage right on small tables. Tabs close.*

Act One

House lights down.

Mind Mangler (*voiceover*) Member of the Tragic Circle. Prepare to be delighted, astounded and amazed, and welcome to the stage the Mind Mangler.

Tabs open. Intro music. **Mind Mangler** *enters. He strikes his pose.*

Mind Mangler I am the Mind Mangler, medal-winning master of the <u>mind</u>.

NB: Throughout the script all underlined '<u>minds</u>' are followed by a pre-recorded echo.

None of you were able to unlock the safe before the show. Please do try again at the end. It's from my dressing room and all my valuables are stuck inside.

Percy *wheels safe off stage.*

Mind Mangler I got to where I am today by learning how to control others, by learning how to manipulate the human <u>mind</u>.

Points at an **Audience Member**.

You there. I want you to think of a colour.

Sound effects: clunk as lights and videotape screen sharply change to orange.

Any colour at all.

He takes an orange out of his pocket before throwing it off stage.

What colour are you thinking of?

THEN EITHER

Audience Member Orange.

Mind Mangler Orange?

Videotape: **Mind Mangler** *saying, 'Blue. Reverse psychology!'*

OR

Audience Member (*e.g. – could be any other colour*)   Blue.

Mind Mangler   Blue?

Videotape: **Mind Mangler** *saying 'Orange'.* **Mind Mangler** *picks up an envelope from the stage left table.*

THEN

Let's try something else. You here, I want you to think of an animal.

Fast Nasal (*voiceover*)   FROG!

An image of a frog flashes up on the screen.

Mind Mangler   Any animal at all.

Fast Nasal (*voiceover*)   FROG!

Another frog image flashes on the screen.

Mind Mangler   Do not let me influence you.

Fast Nasal (*voiceover*)   SAY FROG!

Zoomed-in frog image flashes on the screen.

Mind Mangler   What animal are you thinking of?

THEN EITHER

Audience Member   Frog.

Mind Mangler *pulls a piece of paper 'FORG' from the envelope.*

Mind Mangler   Frog? I knew it!

OR

Audience Member (*e.g. – could be any other animal*)   Toad.

Mind Mangler   A toad?

Mind Mangler *pulls out the piece of paper (reversed) that reads 'NOT FROG'.*

Not frog.

THEN

Mind Mangler   You're like putty in my hands. Let's try someone else. You there. I want you to clear your mind. That was very quick, okay, now, I want you to think of an object.

Sound effects: clock ticking.

Alright, just watch me and think of any object. Watch my hands and face and think of any object. Take your time, sit back, Rolex and watch! Think of any object. Watch. Have you thought of an object?

Audience Member *responds 'Yes'.* **Percy** *passes them a pen and clipboard with paper.*

Mind Mangler   Excellent. Now don't tell anyone what it is but we're going to give you a piece of paper and a pen.

I want you to write down the object on the piece of paper, fold it up and hide it somewhere no one can see it. We'll come back to you later on in the show.

Percy *collects clipboard and exits. Music.*

Mind Mangler   I suffered from severe night terrors from the age of four to age of . . . well, I still get them. But as I've gotten older I've wanted to know . . . Do these dreams have a deeper meaning or am I just as my therapist says 'making her group sessions all about me'. I told my therapist that I believed these dreams were not just dreams, they were in fact premonitions of things to come. She told me I was beyond help and terminated my therapy. Ironically I hadn't seen that coming. But from then on I wanted to be sure I would always remember my premonitions so I began taking pen and paper to bed with me and I soon became a proficient sleep writer.

Videotape: **Mind Mangler** *sleeping whilst writing frantically in bed at night. He tosses and turns violently before coming to a rest.*

Now my prem –

Videotape: **Mind Mangler** *stirs in bed.*

Now –

Videotape: **Mind Mangler** *stirs violently. He falls off the bed with a thump. Footage ends.*

Now my premonitions are the finale of my act. So this morning I woke up, I took my sleep-written premonition and without reading it rolled it up and sealed it inside an airtight jar to prevent spoilage. I locked that jar into this wooden chest which will remain, much like me at the Magic Circle, suspended until further notice.

He gestures to a wooden chest suspended on a rope above the stage.

At the end of the show I will unlock the chest and reveal my premonition. Although I can only do that with the key to the chest and the key to the chest is locked in the safe. I can only unlock the safe with the code and I did make a note of the code, but I didn't want to lose the code so I locked the code in the chest. There is a spare key to the chest in my car . . . But the key to my car is locked in the safe. There is a spare key to my car in my house but my ex-wife changed the locks. So we might not get to it, but in case we do I'd like everyone here in the front row to keep an eye on the chest, make sure nothing happens to it, make sure no one touches it. Don't get distracted and start enjoying the show. Just watch the box for the rest of the evening. Your ticket money will not be refunded.

Music sting.

My senses are different from yours. Though I have but five you shall learn that mine are rather more developed than your own. I have a sense of taste, but it is a strange taste, for I can taste people's first names.

He begins licking the air and senses someone's name. **Percy** *enters with a chalk board and chalk.* **Mind Mangler** *writes on the board (the audience can't yet see what he's written).*

Mind Mangler   You here, please, nice and clearly for all the audience to hear, what is your name?

Audience Member *response, e.g. 'Nigel'. NB: If it is a 'John' straight away, move straight to 'I knew it'.*

Mind Mangler   Nigel. Are there any Johns in?

If a John volunteers themselves **Mind Mangler** *turns the board around to reveal the word 'JOHN' and moves to 'I knew it'. If not he proceeds with this dialogue until the* **Audience Member** *says yes.*

Mind Mangler   Nigel. Are there any Johns in your immediate family? No? Are there any Johns in your extended family? No? Have you got any friends called John? Have you ever met a John?

Audience Member   Yes.

Mind Mangler   I knew it!

Percy *collects the chalk board.*

Mind Mangler   This is not my only skill. I also have a sense of smell, but it is a strange smell, for I can smell what your job is. When you arrived at the theatre this evening you congregated in the lobby outside, I was secreted in that lobby. I smelt every one of you and from that I was able to detect what your professions are. As I detected them I wrote them down, and now the time has come for me to reveal them. You here, please, what is your job?

Audience Member *responds, e.g. 'lawyer'.* **Mind Mangler** *takes one of several papers from his pocket that is the closest match to the* **Audience Member***'s job. He has cards that read 'INDOORS', 'OUTDOORS', 'DULL', 'SMUG', 'VAGUE JOB', 'OLD', 'MIDWIFE', 'RIDICULOUS', 'EMPLOYED', and 'JUDGE'. He does this with various other members of the audience always trying to best describe the job with the limited and fixed papers in his pockets.*

After he reveals a job he will often make a comment such as 'pretty close' or 'spooky' or moves to 'I knew it'. If the first job he asks for takes place indoors this should be the starting point for the routine. At some point **Mind Mangler** *says, 'Why haven't any of you got normal jobs? Butcher, baker, cobbler, these are normal jobs – what, you don't think there's a cobbler in? Any cobblers in?' etc.*

This is not my only skill. The time has come to reveal my penis. I'm so sorry, no. I do apologise. It's absolutely not time for that. I'm so sorry that's Gene on the teleprompter having a laugh at my expense. Please. Please. The time has come to reveal . . . my sense of hearing, for it is a strange hearing, for I can hear the thoughts of playing cards. I hear them in my <u>mind</u>.

I need a member of the audience to come up and join me on stage. Anyone? Anyone? Anyone?

He ignores anyone from the audience who tries to volunteer. NB: If someone puts their hand up quickly **Mind Mangler** *responds, 'Too keen. Anyone else?' After a beat of silence . . .*

Steve   I'll do it.

Steve *puts up his hand and starts to move through the auditorium.*

Mind Mangler   Yes, you sir, thank you very much. Give him a big hand as he joins me on stage.

Music. **Steve** *goes to the stage trying too hard to appear casual. He is wearing a T-shirt with 'AUDIENCE MEMBER' printed on it.*

Mind Mangler   Thank you very much, sir, now can you please confirm we've never met before?

Steve   No. We do not live together.

Mind Mangler   That's . . . right. What a strange thing to say. Alright. Have you ever been on stage before?

Steve   Only at the rehearsal.

Mind Mangler   Alright, what's your name?

Steve   . . . Steve.

Mind Mangler   Steve, right –

Steve   No, Brian isn't it, we said Brian.

Mind Mangler   Thank you, Brian.

Steve   I'm a [*profession that came up earlier or a combination of a few of them*].

Mind Mangler   Thank you, Brian. Now I want you to think of a card.

Steve   Three of clubs.

Mind Mangler   No! Think of a card, don't say it out loud.

Steve (*whispers*)   Three of clubs.

Mind Mangler   NO! Think of a card, in your <u>mind</u>.

(*To tech box.*) Not that one. Think of a card in your head! Not the three of clubs, that won't work.

Steve   Why?

Mind Mangler   Because you've told me what it is. Think of a different card.

Steve   Four of clubs.

Mind Mangler   No don't say it out loud! Do not say it out loud. Think of a card.

Steve   In my brain?

Mind Mangler   If you have one. Not the three of clubs, not the four of clubs and don't say it, right?

Steve   Right.

Mind Mangler   Right.

Audience Member (*voice from the house*)   Five of clubs.

Mind Mangler   Not the five of clubs! Shut up over there!

Steve   It was! It was the five of clubs. Wooahh!

Mind Mangler   No. Not woah.

Steve   She knew.

Mind Mangler   She didn't know.

Steve   It's like having Debbie McGee in.

Mind Mangler   It's not Debbie McGee in.

Steve   She's proper good she is.

Mind Mangler   She's not good.

Steve   She's better than you are.

Mind Mangler   She's not better than me.

Steve   Yeah she is.

Mind Mangler   What? You think this is easy?

Steve   Yeah, I do actually. Watch this.

Points to the back of the house.

You, what's your job? Shanananana! Theatre usher. Right next –

Mind Mangler   Stop it!

Steve   You're losing your cool.

Mind Mangler   I'm not losing my cool!

Steve   You are.

Mind Mangler   Just . . . never <u>mind</u>. Stop it alright! You all think this is easy, do you?

Audience Member/s *shout 'yes'. If not,* **Steve** *continues . . .*

Steve   Of course they do, look at them all nodding down there.

Mind Mangler   Alright fine you think this is easy? Yeah you've changed your mind now haven't you?

Now you've realised it's interactive. What's your name, down here at the front?

Audience Member *responds, e.g. 'Rachel'.*

Mind Mangler   Rachel, I knew it. Alright, Rachel, if you think it's so easy, you try. I'm going to think of a number, a number between one and ten, okay, Rachel? So why don't you tell me, if it's so easy, what number am I thinking of?

Audience Member *responds with a number, e.g. 'eight'.*

Mind Mangler   Eight. Well, that time it was eight yes, but don't –

Steve   Woah! She read your mind.

Mind Mangler   No! No! It's a one in ten. Anyone can do a one in ten.

Steve   You couldn't.

Mind Mangler   Of course I could, think of a number between one and ten.

Steve   Alright.

Mind Mangler   Three?

Steve   No.

Mind Mangler   Fuck me. Alright we'll try something else. You. What's your name?

Audience Member *responds with their name. If their name is John, then . . .*

Mind Mangler   John? Where were you earlier! I was looking for a John wasn't I? Ten minutes I was looking for a John! I had to put up with a guy who (*ad lib based on first* **Audience Member**).

Steve   I like this guy.

Mind Mangler   I don't like this guy.

Steve   This is a great audience.

Mind Mangler   This is a terrible audience.

He grabs the chalk board again.

Alright, John. John! For God's sake. Right, John, I'm going to think of a colour this time. Give me the board! Give me the board! I'll write it down.

He writes a colour on the board, hidden from the audience.

And if it's so easy to read <u>minds</u> –

(*To tech box.*) Stop it. Not now please. If it's so easy to read <u>minds</u> –

(*To tech box.*) Stop it! Alright! COME ON! If it's so easy to read . . . my thoughts then why don't you tell me, John, what colour am I thinking of.

Audience Member *responds with a colour, e.g. green.*

Mind Mangler   Green?

He turns the board around to reveal the colour he has written matches the audience's selection.

Well it is green, yes! Alright, just stop it! Get off stage now, off stage.

Steve   How did you do that? It's a house full of magicians! QUALITY!

Music. **Steve** *exits into the wings. Spotlight on* **Mind Mangler** *as music stops.*

Mind Mangler   This is not my only skill. Please. Gene, move the teleprompter to the next section. Good. Right. I'd now like to say that it is an honour to be performing for all of you tonight. Not you, but everyone else and I wouldn't be here without my producer. Who is none other than the legendary Bob Kojack.

What, none of you have ever heard of Bob Kojack? Bob Kojack is a massive producer. After this he's got me doing Capital Cruises. They've got twenty-eight ships. Twenty-seven now actually. God rest their souls. So laugh all you want. It's actually a very big opportunity. I'll be performing on a luxury cruise liner. I'll finish my gig then head on down to the cocktail lounge . . . start my twelve-hour shift there and then I am done for the day after that. It's a good gig. I get paid, I get my own bunk and it's a captive audience. I perform in the restaurant, so if they want to eat they have to watch. The point is Bob believes in me, he's invested in my act. He bought me these lights, paid for the set, sent me an extra small silk kimono – that was misjudged – but the point is he believes in me and he's said after Capital Cruises he's sending me to do a show in Las Vegas. (*Reacting to 'ooh'.*) Correct response.

Anyway until then I am touring this show across the UK, so Bob's putting me up in hotels.

Videotape shows map of the UK showing a theatre icon at the location of the theatre and 'cancelled' icons at fifteen other locations across the UK.

He emailed me saying the show's on in Piccadilly, where do you wanna stay? I emailed back just saying nearby.

Unfortunately he misread that email and so I'm staying in the village of Nearby.

Videotape projection of map of the UK showing Nearby (which is far away from the location of the theatre).

Videotape projection – poster for 'MIND MANGLER: MEMBER OF THE TRAGIC CIRCLE'.

So anyway, this show is 'Mind Mangler: Member of the Tragic Circle'. That should say 'Magic Circle' obviously. That's a typo that has appeared on all my posters this year which occurred after using a printing company owned by my ex-wife's sister Jane. My other tours are 'Mind Mangler: Mentalist at Large'.

Videotape: poster for 'MIND MANGLER: MENTALIST WHO IS LARGE'.

You can also see me in 'Mind Mangler: An Evening of Wonder'.

Videotape: poster for 'MIND MANGLER: AN EVENING OF WANKER'.

And of course 'Mind Mangler: The Grand Illusion'.

Videotape: poster with a picture of **Mind Mangler** *and the title 'KNOB'.*

Special effects: musical spike.

Mind Mangler   In this theatre tonight I have demonstrated my ability to manipulate reality but I will now take those powers outside the theatre. This is a live feed of Niagara Falls.

Videotape: a recording of Niagara Falls plays.

Freeze!

The recording is paused.

Unreal. But what is real? After all reality is nothing more than our perception. Is the glass half full or half empty? Am I a sad, divorced man or am I a single man who just happens to cry a lot? Did my ex-wife take the house or did she unburden me of my material possessions . . . and my dog? The point is, there are different ways of looking at things and your perception can be very different from reality.

Percy *enters with camera and we show a live feed of* **Mind Mangler** *on the videotape screen.*

You decide . . . am I really tearing up the pages of this ordinary newspaper?

Music.

Mind Mangler *picks up a copy of* The Daily Telegraph *from the stage left table. He turns the pages to prove it's an ordinary newspaper. As he does he reveals the following headlines and articles within the paper:*

1 – 'CAPITAL CRUISES THREE MORE SHIPS GO DOWN' (COVER)

2 – An image of **Mind Mangler** *with the words 'AWFUL SHOW'*

3 – A headline 'UNATTENDED KILN BURNS DOWN VILLAGE'

4 – A quarter-page advert for his show – 'KNOB' (BACK COVER)

5 – A heavily circled advert for 'CHEAP DIVORCE LAWYERS'.

Mind Mangler *tears and squares up the newspaper. Then with a flourish he reveals the pieces of paper are now back together. Music concludes.*

Mind Mangler   I am now going to manipulate the mind of one member of the audience by creating a psychic bond.

Music spike.

This technique was first pioneered in the early 1900s by Hungarian mentalist and ornithologist Yamrik Putarak –

Videotape shows a black and white image of **Steve** *in Victorian clothing as Yamrick Puterack.*

– who bonded his mind with various birds. At first it was easy, a swan here, an egret there, but he became careless and lost control of the bond. He developed an uncontrollable craving for seed and every winter he found himself inexplicably wandering south. He was eventually arrested for defecating on a car.

Can I have a volunteer from the audience to form a psychic bond with me. You, please come up and join me on stage.

An **Audience Member** *is brought up on stage.*

Mind Mangler   What's your name?

Audience Member *responds, e.g. Sarah.*

Mind Mangler   Sarah, I'm sensing that you are a Sagittarius, is that correct?

He holds a microphone to their mouth.

Mind Mangler (*voiceover*)   Yes.

Mind Mangler   Impossible knowledge. And now, Sarah, I want you to . . . sleep.

*He gets the **Audience Member** to put their head down. Their spotlight goes blue. If they laugh etc. or move **Mind Mangler** reminds them they are asleep: 'Don't laugh, you're asleep', etc.*

Are you asleep, Sarah?

Audience Member *responds, e.g. 'Yes'.*

Mind Mangler   Don't say yes if you're asleep.

Or if they don't respond: 'Well done you've passed the test.'

Now you're falling deeper and deeper into a slumber. The moon shines down.

Light effects: crescent moon gobo appears on the stage-right side of the curtain behind.

The night owl hoots.

Special effects: drum roll and cymbal crash.

Mind Mangler   Now Sarah, a psychic bond is beginning to form between the two of us. You are the glove and I am the hand. You are the cup and I am the water. You are the puppet and I am the . . . hand again. When you wake up our psychic bond will be complete. Now wake up for me, Sarah, stand up.

*He claps. **Percy** enters with A4 pad and marker pen.*

Mind Mangler   We're going to give you a piece of paper and a pen and I want you to write down any number between one and five. Nice and big on the paper. Any number between one and five and because of our psychic bond I will know the number you're thinking of is . . .

Audience Member *writes.* **Percy** *looks over their shoulder and coughs the same number of times as the number written. If the* **Audience Member** *looks at* **Percy** *then* **Mind Mangler** *says: 'Don't look at him, look at me.'*

Mind Mangler (*e.g.*)   Four! Was it a four? Four!

He shows the paper.

Yes, four! Now please, Sarah, write down any one of the primary colours please. That's red, blue or yellow. I don't normally give the list but I think on this occasion it perhaps might be wise. I'm sensing the primary colour you're thinking of is . . .

Audience Member *writes.* **Percy** *looks over their shoulder and puts on a baseball cap in the corresponding colour.*

Mind Mangler   Blue! Is it blue? Yes it's blue!

He shows the paper again.

Now finally, Sarah, I want you to write down any word in the English language. Not just cat or dog, that's too easy, a nice complicated word.

Audience Member *writes a word. (Sign held up in the wings to make them write 'SQUIRREL'.)* **Percy** *looks over their shoulder, unzips his hoodie to reveal the alphabet written on his T-shirt.* **Percy** *uses both hands to quickly point to a complex series of eight or nine letters.*

Dee . . . Dean . . . Deans . . . Deacon!

Deacon!

Percy *takes out a hand-held mirror and holds it over the* **Audience Member***'s shoulder.* **Mind Mangler** *grabs the pad and reads.*

Squirrel! I was close. Round of applause for Sarah as you go back to your seat.

Percy *strikes the chair and microphone and* **Steve** *dressed as a large squirrel enters and takes the pen and pad away.*

Mind Mangler   Now with Sarah we have dipped our toes into the plunge pool of persuasion, but now it's time to dive headfirst into the hot tub of hypnosis.

Sound effects: musical spike.

He puts on some dark goggles with swirly lenses.

I shall now hypnotise the entire audience. Drum roll please.

Sound effects: owl hooting.

I want every single one of you to look into my eyes . . . and SLEEP!

Claps and holds his hands out.

It's not working. Release the sleeping gas!

Two smoke machines blast smoke into the audience.

Mind Mangler   No, no! That's the smoke machine. They're always getting those confused. Sorry. Many people are sceptical about the power of hypnosis but tonight I shall prove once and for all the power I can have on the human brain.

Mind Mangler (*voiceover*)   Ind . . . ind . . . ind . . .

Mind Mangler   I need another randomly selected member of the audience to come up and join me. So whoever catches this ball please make your way up onto the stage.

He pretends to throw a ball out into the crowd, hiding it under his arm. **Steve** *stands up in the crowd holding a duplicate ball.*

Steve   Got it!

Mind Mangler   Yes, you sir! Give him a round of applause!

Steve *runs up onto the stage. We see he is now wearing a T-shirt that reads 'DIFFERENT AUDIENCE MEMBER'.*

Mind Mangler   Hello, sir.

He throws his ball off stage.

What's your name?

Steve   John. (*Callback to previous John here.*)

Mind Mangler   Your name is Mike. Now sit down.

Steve *sits down and immediately goes to sleep.*

Mind Mangler   No, don't go to sleep yet.

Steve   Oh sorry.

Mind Mangler   Wait until I tell you to go to sleep. In this box is my grandfather's antique pocket watch –

He opens a wooden box and sees it's empty.

Someone's had that. Unbelievable.

He searches his pockets.

This is my grandfather's antique –

He finds a plastic spoon in his pocket and reveals it.

– plastic spoon and he could use this spoon to send weak-willed individuals into a deep trance. Watch the plastic spoon, Mike, and sleep.

Steve *falls asleep. If the audience applaud* **Steve** *bows.*

Mind Mangler   Now, Mike, every time you shake my hand you will be compelled to reveal a deeply held personal secret. When I clap my hands you will wake up and jump to your feet.

He claps his hands twice.

Mike! Stand!

Percy *enters with a mic stand.*

Mind Mangler   NOT THAT! GET OFF WITH THAT!

(*To* **Steve**.) Get up!

Steve   My secret is –

Mind Mangler   No, no, wait until I shake your hand.

They shake hands.

Now!

Steve   You have IBS.

Mind Mangler   No! That's my personal secret! Tell me one of your personal secrets.

Steve   Oh, right, sorry.

They shake hands.

My colleague has IBS.

Mind Mangler   GO BACK TO SLEEP!

Steve *sleeps.*

Now, Mike, it's time to have a bit of fun. When I ring this bell you will become . . . a horse.

Mind Mangler *rings the bell.*

Steve (*with a hoarse voice*)   Oh wow, I've been hypnotised.

Mind Mangler   What is wrong with you?

Steve (*still hoarse*)   I don't know but I could use a lozenge.

Mind Mangler   We're going to be here all night!

Steve *takes out a pocket watch and checks the time.*

Steve   Yeah we're already running behind.

Mind Mangler   That's my pocket watch!

He snatches the pocket watch and puts it in a case.

I've told you before, you are not allowed to touch my grandfather's pocket watch. You are not a magician.

He goes to take out the pocket watch and finds the case empty.

Where's the pocket watch?!

Steve *takes it out of his pocket.*

Steve   I dunno how I've done that.

Mind Mangler *snatches it back again. He swings the pocket watch between them.*

Mind Mangler   Give me that! Now repeat after me: You will obey my every command.

Both   You will obey my every command. You will obey my every command.

Mind Mangler *falls asleep.*

Steve   What he's done now?

He prods the **Mind Mangler** *and tries to rouse him.*

Steve   Alright, I'll step in . . . from now on, when you shake hands you'll give away a personal secret and when I ring the bell you'll become . . . Someone give us an animal?

Audience Member/s *respond, e.g. 'Chicken'.*

Steve   Yep, a chicken.

He rings the bell.

Mind Mangler   Bukaaaw!

He falls back asleep.

Steve   Very good. Let's try some more.

He gets a few suggestions and plays around. Eventually he chooses a final animal, the more unusual the better. **Mind Mangler** *does his best to imitate this animal.*

Alright, so when you shake hands, you're gonna give away a personal secret, when I ring this bell, you're gonna become [*final animal*]. Quality. Now when I clap my hands, you'll wake up and think it's gone brilliantly.

He claps. **Mind Mangler** *wakes up.*

Mind Mangler   Thank you very much, give him a round of applause.

He shakes **Steve**'s *hand.*

I have IBS.

Sound effects: music.

Chorus (*voiceover; gospel choir*)   Quickfire Jesus!

Tight spotlight up on **Mind Mangler**. *He shows the audience a bottle of water.*

Mind Mangler   Water!

He shakes it. He reveals it has turned into a bottle of wine.

Wine!

Sound effects: angelic singing.

Chorus (*voiceover*)   Quickfire Jesus!

Lights return to normal. Tabs close.

Mind Mangler   Now it's time to return to our volunteer who thought of an object earlier on in the show. Don't tell anyone what it is. I just want you to focus on your object.

Sound effects: clock ticking.

Mind Mangler (*voiceover*)   Watch. Watch. Watch. Watch. Watch.

Mind Mangler   Now, was your object . . . a watch?

Audience Member   No.

Mind Mangler   No?

Sound effects: short fanfare.

A kabuki drop falls revealing the word 'WATCH'.

Mind Mangler   Not a watch? A clock? No. Well, we'll come back to you later. A sun dial! Yes. No. We'll come back to you later.

Music. Kabuki flies out.

Mind Mangler   Now I shall demonstrate that not only am I mentally superior to all humans but also superior to sophisticated technology. Join me as I compete against computers in Mind versus Machine.

Music. Tabs open to reveal a trolley with four large jars on it, each containing a brain, preserved in alcohol.

These are some of the greatest minds who ever lived. A physicist, an engineer, a concert pianist and a biochemist. All four were donated to medical science, but I got them. This screen is connected to a I63 Max Super Computer with a processing speed of one hundred and ten gigahertz per second. It has been programmed to do one thing and one thing alone. To play chess!

A digital chess board appears on the videotape screen. **Mind Mangler** *puts on a swim-cap-style hat with cables running from it to the four jars. Sound effects: computer powering up.*

It has already beaten sixteen grand masters. But can it beat my super-powered brain? Let's play!

Sound effects: dramatic competition music begins.

Pawn to F3.

The white pawn moves to F3 and the computer immediately responds with the black pawn moving to E5.

Pawn to G4.

Another white pawn moves to G4 and the computer immediately responds and the black queen moves to H4. A pop-up message on the screen reads 'CHECKMATE. YOU LOSE.'

Move on to the next test.

A large Minesweeper game screen appears.

Mind Mangler *immediately hits a mine and all the mines on the screen explode. Sound effects: 90s computer explosion.*

He sadly takes off his hat and wheels the trolley off into the stage-right wing. Loud sound of glass smashing stage right.

Mind Mangler   We have now reached a serious point in tonight's proceedings. All my life I have been lied to. By my wife about her lovers, by my father about his lovers, and by my vicar about his relationship with my wife and my father. However, recently while lamenting exactly these issues in an internet chatroom for high-profile men on low incomes I met a man who taught me how to detect any lie. So I am now a spier of liars, a perceiver of deceivers, a rooter-outer of untruth-spouters and the time has come for me to reveal your –

Videotape screen (now displaying a swirling hypnotic image) freezes and jumps with an error sound. The image changes to display a web browser with a Google search . . . 'How to sell tickets fast.'

Oh no, close the browser please.

Videotape: The tab closes to reveal another Google search . . . 'How do I stop IBS?'

Not just the tab, the browser.

Videotape: The tab closes to reveal another search . . . 'How to sell tickets urgently.'

No, that's just the tab, close the whole browser!

Videotape: The tab closes to reveal another search . . . 'Who is Bob Kojack? – No Results Found'

No, you're only closing the tab, close the whole browser!

Videotape: The tab closes to reveal a website 'Rent-A-Crowd.com'.

No! CLOSE THE WHOLE BROWSER!

Videotape: The browser closes to reveal **Mind Mangler**'s *computer desktop. The background image is his wedding photo. The cursor clicks on a file which restores the swirling video.*

It's time to expose your secrets. First I need to tune in to your thoughts. This is the human radio.

Musical sting. **Percy** *brings* **Mind Mangler** *some large headphones and a metel detector-style device.*

Mind Mangler   Using my patented mind wave receiving device I am able to listen to your thoughts.

He walks into the crowd followed by **Percy** *on camera; a live feed comes up on the videotape screen.* **Mind Mangler** *hovers his detector over the heads of the* **Audience Members**.

Audience Member One (*voiceover*)   I'm giving this one star on TripAdvisor.

Audience Member Two (*voiceover*)   I hate audience participation.

Audience Member Three (*voiceover*)   (*Yodelling.*)

Mind Mangler *retracts the device and the yodelling stops. He holds it above their head again and the yodelling plays.* **Mind Mangler** *moves on.*

Audience Member Four (*voiceover; male*)   I think my wife's sleeping with her French teacher.

Audience Member Five (*voiceover; female*)   I am.

Audience Member Six (*voiceover; male*)   Bonjour.

Mind Mangler *retreats.*

Mind Mangler   I am tuned in to your thoughts. When you arrived here tonight many of you wrote down a secret on one of these cards. Maybe you committed a crime. Maybe you know someone who committed a crime. Maybe you discovered your ex-wife was sleeping with David Blaine and you spent three days secretly filming them together to prove it to the divorce arbitrator and didn't realise that was a crime. You placed your secret into one of these glass bowls which have remained in full view for the whole performance. It's time to choose a secret from the bowl. Who haven't we spoken to yet?

He takes one of the glass bowls containing the audience's written secrets. He holds it out to an **Audience Member**.

Mind Mangler   Can you please pick a card and read the name but not the secret. Just the name, not the secret.

Audience Member *responds, e.g. Samantha Banks.*

Mind Mangler   Samantha Banks, do we have a Samantha Banks in the audience?

He finds the **Audience Member**. *The following section is improvised based on the nature of the secret.* **Mind Mangler** *correctly predicts the secret.*

Second round of this with a second real secret.

Final time **Mind Mangler** *has another* **Audience Member** *select a final card from one of the bowls.*

Again the name but not the secret please.

The **Audience Member** *explains there is no name on this card, just the secret.*

No name . . . okay . . . is there a . . . check the back, sometimes people write stuff on the back. No name at all? Is there a secret? Yes. Right, read out the secret and we'll work out who it belongs to.

Audience Member (*reads*)   My best friend got offered a dream job abroad, but they couldn't go because I forgot to post their visa application.

Mind Mangler   All of a sudden the lack of name makes complete sense. Everyone stand up.

Improvised section: we continue to eliminate people until there are only four or five remaining.

Alright, you're all now going to say the same thing . . . that is not my secret.

Audience Member   That is not my secret.

All but one member of the audience are eliminated.

Mind Mangler   So that means our culprit must be . . .

Steve *is the only person left standing.*

Mind Mangler   For God's sake.

Steve   That is not my secret!

Mind Mangler   You! Wait . . . you didn't post my visa application?

Steve   No. I'm sorry, mate.

Mind Mangler   I thought you sent it off like two months ago.

Steve (*possible improv here linking the reason for not posting the visa to one of the secrets*)   I meant to do it! But I forgot and then I found it yesterday in the bottom of my backpack and then I was gonna send it off but I realised it was covered in yogurt.

Mind Mangler   But I need that visa to do my gig in Las Vegas.

Steve   Yeah.

Mind Mangler   That's the Bob Kojack gig, the gig's in like six weeks and the visa takes . . .

Steve   Three months to go through . . . I'm so sorry, mate.

Mind Mangler   You've ruined it. You've ruined the show tonight and now you've ruined my whole career.

Steve   Look, just let me explain . . .

Mind Mangler   No, forget it. Got a show to do.

Steve *exits the auditorium.*

Mind Mangler   I have never been so completely undermined. STOP IT! We'll do the Act One finale.

Tabs close.

Mind Mangler   I recently spent the majority of my life savings on an antique, glass vanishing cabinet once used by Victorian magician Robert Moulin. Unfortunately we are unable to use it this evening for technical reasons. Which reminds me, if you exit through the main doors, please do be careful, there is a lot of broken glass out there. However, the bar manager here at the Apollo has supplied us with an alternative. This is the glass vanishing cabinet.

Tabs open to reveal a plugged in, glass-fronted freezer. One shelf remains inside at the top with a few rows of ice cream.

Just as Robert Moulin did two hundred years ago I shall enter the vanishing cabinet.

He turns and walks to the freezer. He struggles to get inside. He is obviously very cold inside.

After entering the cabinet Robert Moulin's assistant would lock the door from the outside.

Percy *enters and locks the door with a small key.*

Mind Mangler   Once locked inside Robert Moulin would turn around to demonstrate all four sides of the cabinet are solid.

He stands a little and tips the shelf above his head, the ice creams falling all over him.

Ah! And then Robert Moulin would vanish in a puff of smoke!

Thick smoke pours into the freezer.

No, that's the sleeping gas!

He passes out and flops against the glass front.

Videotape: the word 'Interval' appears with a clunk.

Blackout. Tabs close.

Interval.

During Interval

Mind Mangler (*voiceover*)   This is the Mind Mangler. In the second half of the show, I will perform an experiment using ninety-six Rubik's Cubes. Before the second act begins, please come up onto the stage and mix one of the Rubik's Cubes as much as you'd like and place it in a random location in the grid.

Act Two

Lights down.

Mind Mangler (*voiceover*)   Please welcome back to the stage . . . the Mind Mangler.

Music. Tabs open. **Mind Mangler** *enters.*

Mind Mangler   I hope you enjoyed the interval, I've been told by many it is a highlight of the show. That's Gene on the teleprompter again, sorry. What did we just discuss in the interval? Next up, my arse GENE!

Now, there are fifty-two cards in a standard deck. We're going to choose just one. We'll start with you, would you like to choose a high card or a low card?

Audience Member *responds, e.g. high.*

Mind Mangler   High, I knew it.

Mind Mangler *takes out an envelope with a downward facing arrow on it. He quickly turns the arrow up the other way.*

I knew it. A high card. Which high card would you like the 10, Jack, Queen or King?

Audience Member *responds, e.g. Queen.*

Mind Mangler *takes a smaller envelope out of the larger envelope.*

Mind Mangler   The Queen and is there any way I could have known you would say Queen?

Audience Member   No.

Mind Mangler *turns the envelope to reveal the word 'No'.*

Mind Mangler   No. Very good. And finally you here I want you to choose a suit.

Hearts, clubs, diamonds or spades which would you like?

Audience Member *responds, e.g. Clubs.*

Mind Mangler   Clubs. You have chosen the Queen of Clubs and that is amazing because before the show I placed into this envelope the . . .

Mind Mangler *opens the envelope to reveal a folded piece of paper. Mind Mangler reads what it says.*

'Hi Keith, its Steve, sorry I took your playing card. My deck was short for poker night.'

Mind Mangler *looks annoyed and glares into the wings, the camera pans and we see* **Steve** *in the wings holding a piece of paper with 'I'm sorry' written on it.*

Mind Mangler *signals for* **Steve** *to leave and he trudges off with his sign.*

'But didn't want to mess up your show so left you this note on the back of a flyer for a tennis club.'

Mind Mangler *unfolds the paper and reads again.*

'Sign up for a year's membership at Queen's Club.' Queen's Club! Queen's Club, that's the Queen of Clubs!

Sound effects: triumphant musical sting.

For the last decade I have spent three hours a day practising the game Rock Paper Scissors. When my wife left me I built this device so I could remain match fit.

Percy *wheels on a spinning wheel device made from an old bicycle wheel with a rock, a pad of paper and a pair of scissors attached.*

Let's play!

Sound effects: music. **Mind Mangler** *spins the wheel and holds out a hand (paper). The wheel slowly stops on scissors.*

Chorus (*voiceover*)   Quickfire Jesus.

A box on a table is wheeled on. **Mind Mangler** *tips it over to show it's empty.*

Mind Mangler   Empty!

He tips it back up.

Loaf! Fishes!

He throws in a loaf of bread and two fish.

Loaves and fishes!

He upends the box and hundreds of loaves and fishes fall out.

Chorus (*voiceover*)   Quickfire Jesus.

Tabs close. **Mind Mangler** *turns back to the* **Audience Member** *who suggested the object.*

Mind Mangler   Scissors?

Audience Member   No.

Mind Mangler   No. We'll come back to you later.

Sound effects: musical sting.

Since my divorce I've found myself with a lot of time on my hands and I've been putting that time and my hands to good use. Four times a day I lock myself in my bedroom, lubricate my hands and do something I am now going to do in front of all of you. Solve a Rubik's Cube.

He takes out a Rubik's Cube.

This Rubik's Cube is, much like my TripAdvisor reviews, mixed. Behold!

He turns around. Sound effects: Rubik's Cube shuffling. **Mind Mangler** *reveals the cube is now completed.*

Impossible. How do –

He raises his hands and the mixed Rubik's Cube falls out from where he placed it under his arm. He quickly throws them both into the wings.

How do I do it? Throughout the interval many of you mixed a Rubik's Cube and placed it in a random location in the grid. There are still three spaces in the grid so I now need three members of the audience to come up and join me on stage.

He brings up three people. Music.

Now it may appear that I have selected three random members of our audience but in fact they all have something in common. Today is all three of your birthdays. Is that correct?

Mind Mangler *walks past them all holding out the mic.*

Mind Mangler (*voiceover*)   Yes. Yes. Yes.

Mind Mangler   Happy birthday!

He brings on a microphone stand and hand held microphone and greets them, shaking their hands in turn as asking their names.

Let's meet our volunteers. What's your name?

He shakes each audience member's hand, revealing a different secret about himself each time.

I have IBS. I avoid tax. I hit something on the way here with my car and kept driving.

In a moment I'm going to get you to mix up a Rubik's Cube, but first of all I want you to take a card and pass them along the row. We're going to give you a pen as well and you're going to write down a word, but not just any word, you're going to write down a word that I am going to beam into your brain. Everyone standing by with your pen? I'm going to transmit the word, NOW.

Sound effects: crackling electricity.

Don't overthink it, just write down the first word that came into your head. Now during the interval many of you came up onstage and mixed up a Rubik's Cube and placed it in a random location in the grid. Give me a cheer if you did that? Thank you very much. Now you may have thought all those decisions of how to mix the cube and where to place it were random, but in the interval we were playing this music.

Sound effects: interval music plays briefly.

And what happens if we play the interval music backwards!

Sound effects: backwards music with **Mind Mangler***'s voice woven in.*

Mind Mangler (*voiceover*)   Left a bit! Bit more! Turn the top! Twice! Stop there! Put it in! Put it in! Top left! Go back to your seat!

Mind Mangler   You have been subliminally influenced. I'm going to collect in your cards, please hold them face down, so I can't see your words. Now you on the end you're going to choose which of these we use. I'm going to mix these up, choose whichever you like.

Happy with that one, you can change your mind if you'd like. You're happy with that one, wonderful. I'm going to place that on this stand in full view throughout the experiment.

He places the card in a stand on the table.

Now I want all of you to choose one of these Rubik's Cubes. Whichever you like.

He offers them a bowl of Rubik's Cubes. Each **Audience Member** *takes a cube.*

Mind Mangler   There you go. Please mix your cubes now!

Sound effects: music. **Mind Mangler** *goes to the Rock Paper Scissors wheel and spins it again, holding out his hand (rock). The wheel stops on paper.*

Mind Mangler (*irritated*)   Right, you've mixed up your cubes. We're gonna put them in the grid. We've got three spaces left. One, two and three.

He takes each cube from each **Audience Member** *and places it in the grid where they'd like it to go before sending them back to their seat.*

Mind Mangler   Now you mixed up these cubes, you chose where they went. Three random people, three random words, we shuffled, we chose. All of that appears impossible to predict.

Videotape: live camera feed, a close-up shot of the Rubik's Cube grid and the card in the stand in front of it.

Except somehow I knew that the word that one of you would write down when you looked into my eyes would be . . .

He turns the card in the stand around to reveal the word 'TOSSER'. Videotape: camera zooms in on the card.

Tosser!

Videotape: close-up shot of the card with 'TOSSER' written on it.

Right, well, the joke's on you because that's not what the Rubik's Cubes say the Rubik's Cubes say . . .

He turns the table around to reveal the other side of the Rubik's Cube grid. The cubes have created a mosaic image of the **Mind Mangler** *with the word 'TOSSER' written below.*

Tosser! How dare you!

Percy *pulls the table upstage and the tabs close. Sound effects: music.* **Mind Mangler** *goes to the Rock Paper Scissors wheel and spins it again, holding out his hand (rock). The wheel is about to stop on paper and* **Mind Mangler** *quickly yanks to back so it stops on scissors.*

A normal human uses only 10 per cent of their brain, but according to my doctor I am abnormal. Using my brain's full potential I am able to break down the molecular structure of my own body and transport those atoms through time and space.

Music. Tabs open to reveal two hooped curtains, one of which is already raised. **Mind Mangler** *steps into the lowered hoop stage left.*

Behold!

He raises his curtain. The other curtain lowers to reveal **Steve** *dressed as* **Mind Mangler** *with large fake beard.* **Steve** *mimes as* **Mind Mangler** *speaks.*

Mind Mangler (*off*)   That is the power of the <u>mind</u>.

Steve *walks down to the Rock Paper Scissors wheel and spins it. Sound effects: music.* **Steve** *holds out his hand (paper), the wheel stops on rock.* **Mind Mangler** *lowers his curtain.*

Mind Mangler   OH COME ON!

He raises his curtain. **Steve** *walks back upstage, into his hoop and raises his curtain.* **Mind Mangler** *lowers his again.*

Mind Mangler   Impossible. Thank you very much –

Steve *bows in his hooped curtain.*

Mind Mangler   Thank you very much.

Tabs close.

And now it's time to take a trip to Las Vegas.

Music sting. The sting ends with a cash register bell and **Mind Mangler** *repeats his animal noise from earlier.*

Please. Of course later this year I'll be travelling to Las Vegas for real when I – No, that's not relevant any more. Gene skip that on the teleprompter. Skip that. It has been my dream since I was a child to perform- no skip all that Gene. Yes, good. In several casinos in Las Vegas I am nicknamed the Knob Fish. GENE! In several casinos in Las Vegas I am nick named the Card Shark because I have an unbeatable system for winning at any casino game and I've been lulling casinos in Las Vegas into a false sense of security by losing thousands and thousands of pounds over the last thirty years. I've got them right where I want them.

And I've made all my money back anyway by stealing over two tonnes of complimentary miniature soaps over the years. If anyone would like to purchase some please do get in contact, the storage costs are crippling.

Now where some people can read words I can read . . .
probabilities. I can also read words.

Music. **Percy** *wheels on a table. On the table are three tubes and
three small glasses.*

I'm going to give three members of this audience the chance
to try and out-gamble me in a game, the game is this. I have
here three glasses.

He demonstrates that they are empty.

– into one of the glasses I'm going to place a red envelope
containing twenty of my very own, very last, pounds.

*He takes a twenty-pound note from his wallet and places it into one of
the glasses. He covers the three glasses with tubes and mixes them up.*

I'll cover the glasses and mix them up. If you choose the
glass with the twenty-pound note in it you keep twenty
pounds, if you choose one of the empty glasses I keep the
twenty pounds. You have a chance here, a chance to win, but
of course against me you have no chance as I'm going to be
manipulating your every move. It's time to mix the glasses.

Music. **Mind Mangler** *mixes the glasses.*

We'll play with you. A, B or C? Which one do you think the
money's in? I'll give you a clue. It's in A.

Sound effects: ding. **Mind Mangler** *pushes tube A forward.*

But am I telling the truth or am I bluffing? Which one do
you think it's in?

Audience Member *chooses a tube. Whichever they choose, they are
right.* **Percy** *runs the money to the winning audience member.*

Mind Mangler   You think it's in A? It is in A yes. Fair
enough. Twenty quid. Round of applause. We're going to
play again, so we have to play three times, that's in the
contract. Not a problem. We should have played with tens
but that's fine. Another twenty pounds goes into one of the

glasses. We'll cover them over again and it's time again to mix the glasses.

Music. **Mind Mangler** *mixes the glasses. This time he hides the tubes under his jumper and mixes them up.*

You there. A, B or C? Which one do you think? I'll give you a clue, it's in B.

Sound effects: ding. **Mind Mangler** *pushes tube B forward.*

But am I telling the truth or am I bluffing? Which one do you think it's in?

Audience Member *chooses a tube. Whichever they chose, they are right.*

That is right. I don't know how you've done that. That's another twenty pounds. That's forty quid.

Again **Percy** *runs the money to the winning* **Audience Member**.

Mind Mangler   We'll play again, it's not a problem. Tell you what, this time we're going to play with ten.

He takes out a twenty-pound note from his wallet.

Mind Mangler   I've only got fifty so we'll play with fifty. That's my last fifty quid. I need that to get back to Nearby. Okay, fifty quid, in it goes.

He puts a twenty-pound note into one of the glasses. He covers and mixes them.

We cover those over and it's time once again to mix the glasses.

Music. **Mind Mangler** *mixes the glasses. This time he continues mixing the glasses long after the music finishes.*

Let's play with . . . you! A, B or C? Which one do you think? I'll give you a clue, it's in A, B or C. You think it's in A? That one there. Final answer? Alright I'm going to make it easy for you. I'm going to remove one of them. I'm going to remove C. It's not in C, so it's in A or B. Fifty-fifty and you're saying it's in A, correct?

He switches A and B's position as he says this.

You think it's in that one there?

Wrong I'm afraid! It's not in A! It's not in B! It's not in C! It's back in my wallet!

Music. **Percy** *exits, wheeling off the table.*

Chorus (*voiceover*)   Quickfire Jesus.

Tabs open to reveal a platform made of bottles of mineral water. Music continues. **Mind Mangler** *walks across the platform.*

Chorus (*voiceover*)   Quickfire Jesus.

Tabs close.

Mind Mangler   Thank you very much. The time has come for me to reveal another of my senses. Join me as I touch the dead.

Sound effects: spooky music.

In the next ten minutes I shall be touching one of your dead relatives on stage in front of you.

I recently purchased a Ouija board from an antiques shop on Drury Lane. That night I went to bed and immediately started to hear strange sounds coming from the downstairs room where the board was kept and I suffered terrible nightmares. I decided to return the board but when I went back the next day the shop was gone. They'd turned it into a Greggs. I now need another member of the audience to come up and join me on stage.

Tab opens. **Percy** *enters with the camera and we choose a volunteer.*

Mind Mangler   You there in the orange jacket, would you mind coming up? Big round of applause for our volunteer.

An **Audience Member** *in an orange puffer jacket comes up onto the stage. Tabs close.*

Thank you very much. Would you mind just grabbing the microphone from the wings?

The **Audience Member** *exits stage right and* **Steve** *reenters in the same jacket holding the microphone.*

Thank you sir. Now, what is your name?

Steve *takes out a wallet from the pocket of the jacket and looks at the card.*

Steve   I'm . . . Paul.

Mind Mangler   Paul, good, now tell us something about yourself.

Steve   I bank at Barclays.

Mind Mangler   Very good.

Steve   My long card number is –

Mind Mangler   Thank you.

Steve *takes a loyalty card out of the wallet.*

Steve   I'm a member of the East Ealing Society.

Steve *looks into another pocket.*

And I always carry a sock.

Mind Mangler   Now Paul, I'm sensing you've recently lost your brother. Is that correct?

Steve   Yes.

Mind Mangler   We will now contact your brother using the Ouija board.

The curtains open to reveal a table with a Ouija board on it and two chairs. **Steve** *sits down.*

Sound effects: spooky music.

Mind Mangler   The ghosts of the dead are all around us.
They are among us tonight. You cannot see her but sitting
over there is an elderly woman who has been clearly dead
for many years . . . Oh no I'm so sorry, madam, no I thought
you were . . . No, no I'm so sorry, that's my mistake.
Sometimes it can be hard to tell.

He sits down.

We're now going to contact Paul's brother using the Ouija
board. Paul will act as a conduit between the land of the
living and the domain of the dead. Ring the spirit bell to
open up the gateway!

Steve *rings the bell on the table. The* **Mind Mangler** *repeats the
animal impression from before.*

Now Paul –

Steve *rings the bell on the table again. The* **Mind Mangler** *repeats
the animal impression from before.*

Now Paul –

Steve *rings the bell on the table again. The* **Mind Mangler** *repeats
the animal impression, then moves the bell away from* **Steve***.*

Now Paul, place your hands on the planchette.

After a moment's consideration **Steve** *puts his hands on his head.*

Mind Mangler   No.

Steve *slowly moves his hands towards his crotch.*

Mind Mangler   NO! This.

*He gestures to the planchette and accidentally rings the bell with his
elbow. He repeats the animal impressions again.* **Steve** *moves the
bell away from him.*

Steve *puts his hands on the planchette.*

Mind Mangler   Now, is there anybody there?

Steve *moves planchette to 'NO'.*

Steve   No.

Mind Mangler   No? Then who moved it?!

Steve   Well, I did.

Mind Mangler   No! It was a ghost. Try again: is there anybody there?

Steve *moves planchette.*

Steve *(frustrated)*   Yes.

Mind Mangler   Yes! Good, right.

Sound effects: dramatic musical sting.

What is your name, spirit?

Steve *moves the planchette.*

Steve   P.

Mind Mangler   No.

Steve   A.

Mind Mangler   No.

Steve   U.

Mind Mangler   No, that's your name. You're Paul. The spirit has a different name. What's the spirit's name?

Steve *moves the planchette.*

Steve   P.

Mind Mangler   Jesus.

Steve   R.

Mind Mangler   Okay.

Steve   A.

Mind Mangler   Right.

Steve   U.

Mind Mangler   Fuck me.

Steve   L.

Mind Mangler   Praul?!

Steve   Yeah, me brother Praul. Paul and Praul.

Mind Mangler   Not Praul. Not Paul. A different name.

Steve *moves the planchette again, this time towards the J.*

Mind Mangler   Not John.

Steve *moves the planchette to the L.*

Steve   L.

Mind Mangler   Thank God.

He moves it to the word 'OUIJA' at the top of the board.

Steve   Ouija. Luigi!

Mind Mangler   Luigi. Do you have a message for us?

Steve *moves the planchette to 'NO'.*

Steve   No.

Mind Mangler *snatches it and puts it on 'YES'.*

Mind Mangler   I think he does. I think he definitely does. Otherwise what was the point of all this!? What's the message?

Steve *moves the planchette to I. C. A. N. T.*

I . . . C . . . I see . . . A . . . N . . . I can . . . T . . . I can't.

Steve *moves the planchette to R.E.M.E.*

Mind Mangler   R . . . E . . . M . . . E – You can't remember what you're supposed to do now.

Steve   I'm so sorry.

Mind Mangler   What is wrong with you?! You've ruined every single section you've come up for, you've ruined my chance of performing in Vegas. Bob Kojack's going to think I'm an idiot now.

Steve   No he won't.

Mind Mangler   How would you know?

Steve   Because I am Bob Kojack.

Beat.

Sound effects: dramatic musical sting.

Mind Mangler   Gene!

Steve   That's why you've never met him and it's all been on email.

Mind Mangler   So you were just messing with me this whole time?

Steve   No, it's not like that. You were so down when Amy left. So I wanted to give you a bit of a boost so I made Bob up so I could put some money into your show and give you something to hope for. I didn't mean for it to get out of hand.

Mind Mangler   So you paid for the set?

Steve   Yeah.

Mind Mangler   And you bought me the new lights?

Steve   Yeah.

Mind Mangler   And you sent me the extra-small silk kimono?

Steve   That was for me.

Mind Mangler   I just . . . I don't understand.

Steve   Well, I'm very small and I wanted a kimono.

Mind Mangler   No! I understand that! Of course I understand that. I don't understand why you lied.

Steve   I was just trying to help.

Mind Mangler   Well, you haven't helped. You have not helped. I thought I was off to Vegas. I thought someone actually important believed in me.

Steve   I believe in you.

Mind Mangler   You're not important, you're an embarrassment.

Steve   Sorry, Keith.

Mind Mangler   Don't use my real name. You can't even do that can you? You can't even pretend you're a member of the audience. You're just an idiot.

Steve   You're right. I'm so sorry.

He sadly walks back into the auditorium. Audience react.

Mind Mangler   It's time to bend spoons. This spoon is solid. It is made of stainless steel. You will watch as I interfere with it, and bend it with my psychic power.

He focuses intensely on the spoon and tries to bend it. Nothing happens. He becomes more and more frustrated and tense.

After a minute of nothing we see the microphone stand behind him start to slowly bend. **Mind Mangler** *doesn't notice as it bends completely in half. He continues to focus on the spoon. The festoon arch behind him starts to bend as well. He falls to his knees. A lighting bar bends and the lamps slide to the end of the bar.* **Mind Mangler** *becomes more and more tense, screaming and weeping. Music plays a final flourish.*

And that is the power of the <u>mind</u>.

Improvised section with the audience shouting 'Mind', etc.

What a load of *shit*! Oh come on!

Mind Mangler *takes off his glasses and medal.*

Mind Mangler   Let's do the finale. My French ancestor Pierre Mangler was an aristocrat living in Paris. In 1796 he was executed by guillotine at the hands of a revolutionary mob at the stroke of midnight.

Sound effects: church bell. The **Mind Mangler** *repeats the animal impression. (Optional repeat twelve times.)*

Tonight I will face the same fate but unlike Pierre I will escape.

Tabs open to reveal a large guillotine. **Mind Mangler** *moves downstage right.*

I need two volunteers from the audience to help me with this. You can remain in your seats.

Mind Mangler *selects two people near the front. They are given mics, padlocks and told to stand by the* **Cloaked Figures**.

Mind Mangler   You're going to be given a four-digit combination padlock. What I want you to do is set that four-digit padlock to a random four-digit code of your choosing. We'll show you how to do that.

Audience Members *set the padlocks.*

Mind Mangler   I will be locked into the guillotine using these padlocks. My only path to survival will be to deduce the random codes before this timer runs out and the blade is released. I need one more member of the audience to come up and join me on stage and start the timer. So let's have . . . yes you in the suit . . . round of applause for our volunteer in the suit.

Steve *comes up wearing a checked shirt and suit jacket.*

Mind Mangler   Can you please confirm we have never met before?

Steve   We have never met before.

Mind Mangler   . . . Good. And what's your name?

Steve   Clive.

Mind Mangler   . . . Clive. Good. The guillotine is connected to this timer – when the countdown runs out the rope will be released and the blade will fall. What I need you to do is stand over there and when I give the command push the red button to start the timer and give me an update on how much time has passed every thirty seconds. Have you got that?

Steve   Yeah. Stand over there, press the red button when you say and let you know how much time has elapsed at thirty-second intervals using the timer.

Mind Mangler   You've got that?

Steve   I won't let you down.

Mind Mangler   The executioners will now lock me into the guillotine.

Two **Cloaked Figures** *take* **Mind Mangler***'s jacket and help him into the guillotine.*

Mind Mangler   When the timer starts I will onlyhave ninety seconds to escape or else suffer the fate of Pierre Mangler. The padlocks have been set to random codes.

Let's put them in place.

The **Cloaked Figures** *lock the padlocks onto the guillotine and then exit.*

Mind Mangler   Don't forget to scramble the digits. The padlocks are shut. Ninety seconds on the clock. Start the timer . . . now!

Steve *presses the button and the two-minute countdown begins. Music.* **Mind Mangler** *struggles to figure out the codes. Muttering numbers.*

(*To the first* **Audience Member** *in their seat.*) Volunteer on the right of the auditorium. Visualise your code. I'm sensing the last number is a 2 – is that correct, is that right? Yes? No? Not a 2 at the end?

He discusses the code with the **Audience Member**.

Your code wasn't 1682?

Audience Member   No.

Mind Mangler *fiddles with the lock*.

Mind Mangler   No? Are you Melissa?

Audience Member   No.

Mind Mangler   Did the stage manager come and speak to you during the interval?

Audience Member   No.

Mind Mangler   No?!

Steve   Sixty seconds.

Mind Mangler   Right, so these are just random codes? Okay, that's fine. Visualise your code on this side. Was the final number a 4? No? A 5? No? Was there a 5 in the number? Okay . . . really see each. Really see each digit in your mind's eye.

Steve   You're running out of time.

Mind Mangler   Unhelpful. Just tell me what the code is.

Audience Member (*e.g.*)   7561.

This section will be different each night. If the **Audience Member** *remembers the code* **Mind Mangler** *gets it wrong and berates them; if they don't remember he continues to try and jog their memory. Eventually he manages to open the first lock.*

Mind Mangler   Yes!

(*To the other* **Audience Member**.) Okay, over this side, what was your code?

Audience Member (*prepared*)   I can't remember.

Mind Mangler   You can't remember?

Steve   Thirty seconds.

Mind Mangler   Shit. Steve! I need your help.

Steve   Who's Steve? I'm Clive.

He gives **Mind Mangler** *a knowing thumbs-up.*

Mind Mangler   No, forget that. Deactivate the timer!

Steve   I'm just a member of the audience.

Mind Mangler   Get me out!

Steve   You've got to do it yourself, mate!

Mind Mangler   GET ME OUT OF THE GUILLOTINE!

Steve   Fifteen seconds.

Mind Mangler (*to audience*)   SOMEONE HELP! DO SOMETHING!

A **Cloaked Figure** *runs back on to help.*

Steve   No! No! It's all part of it.

Mind Mangler *manages to unlock the final padlock.*

Mind Mangler   Got it!

He takes off the padlock. The timer runs out. The blade falls cutting off his head. Music cuts out.

Steve   Why are you applauding? Don't worry everyone it's all part of it. Don't worry it's all part . . .

Beat. Edges towards the basket and sees the head.

Ohh shit. Keith, is this a new bit, mate? Cough twice if it's a new bit. No. Right I need some help.

The **Cloaked Figures** *enter and start hoisting up the blade.* **Steve** *picks up a head (fake) and shows it to the audience.*

Steve *drops the fake head in the basket, then picks it up and puts it in place. On the videotape screen we see* **Mind Mangler***'s head being put back in place.*

(To the audience.) John! You can do magic. Clap your hands and see if you can bring him back.

Audience Member *claps.* **Mind Mangler** *(on the screen) snaps back to life.*

Mind Mangler *(recorded)*   Arghhh!

Cloaked Figure   Urgh!

One of the **Cloaked Figures** *(***Mind Mangler***) panics and lets go of the rope, chopping the head off again.*

Steve *(to* **Mind Mangler***)*   What have you done?! You've killed my best friend!

Mind Mangler *takes off his cloak to reveal it's him.*

Mind Mangler   Have I?

He moves downstage triumphantly. Tabs close removing the guillotine from view. **Steve** *follows. They bow twice.*

Mind Mangler   Thank you so much! That was Mind Mangler: Member of –

Steve   Woah! Woah! Whatcha doing? Whatcha doing?

Mind Mangler   Finishing the show.

Steve   You can't finish the show until you've done your finale with the box!

Mind Mangler *looks up at the wooden chest still suspended on a rope above them.*

Mind Mangler   I can't do the box 'cause the key's stuck in the safe.

Steve *takes out a key.*

Steve   It's alright, I had another one cut 'cause I knew you'd lose yours.

Mind Mangler   Thanks . . . I'm sorry about before . . . I shouldn't have called you an idiot, I'm sorry.

Steve   That's okay. I'm sorry I pretended to be Bob Kojack, made you think you were going to play in Las Vegas when you weren't, ruined all your routines tonight and hypnotised you to reveal your personal secrets and pretend to be a [*selected animal*].

Mind Mangler   . . . That's okay.

Steve   Hey. Best friends?

He offers out his hand. **Mind Mangler** *shakes it.*

Mind Mangler   Only friend.

Steve   Let's get this done shall we?

He gives **Mind Mangler** *the key.*

Mind Mangler   Lower the box!

Music. **Steve** *goes over and lowers the wooden chest.* **Mind Mangler** *puts the stage right table underneath it.*

Mind Mangler   Now, you in the front row. You've been watching the box, right? No one's come near it? It's been in full view throughout the entire evening – we're going to bring it down for the first time. I'll unlock the padlock with the key.

He opens the chest, takes out the jar, unscrews it and takes out a roll of paper.

Inside this chest is a glass jar. Inside that jar is a roll of paper. On that roll of paper is a prediction that came to me last night in my nightmares. Now if I can do magic as well as John down here then this prediction will mean something.

He and **Steve** *begin to unravel the scroll of paper. The first couple of feet are just messy scrawlings – we can just about make out the first letter of the name of the first* **Audience Member** *we spoke to . . .*

Well, you've gotta know how to interpret it . . . because that looks like an M and we had a Mike in . . . so that's . . . that's pretty good and that's a K and I'm Keith. Let's see what else we've got. We have a J, an O, an H and an N. A John, yes we did have a John and John thought of the colour green! Yes you did and also we met . . .

They unravel the scroll a bit more. **Mind Mangler** *and* **Steve** *keep unravelling the scroll. The writing on it becomes clearer.* **Mind Mangler** *talks through the scroll which contains predictions of things that happened in that night's show including audience members' jobs, secrets and the word selected during the Rubik's Cube routine and finally the object the* **Audience Member** *thought of at the beginning of the show.*

Mind Mangler   Finally, the object . . . who thought of an object, that was you right? You thought of an object at the beginning of the show. You haven't told anyone what it is. Nice and clearly into the microphone, what was your object?

Audience Member *responds, e.g. kettle.*

Mind Mangler   A kettle! And that is the power of the mind!

Blackout.

Lights up. Curtain call.

End.

Methuen Drama Modern Plays

include

Bola Agbaje
Edward Albee
Ayad Akhtar
Jean Anouilh
John Arden
Peter Barnes
Sebastian Barry
Clare Barron
Alistair Beaton
Brendan Behan
Edward Bond
William Boyd
Bertolt Brecht
Howard Brenton
Amelia Bullmore
Anthony Burgess
Leo Butler
Jim Cartwright
Lolita Chakrabarti
Caryl Churchill
Lucinda Coxon
Tim Crouch
Shelagh Delaney
Ishy Din
Claire Dowie
David Edgar
David Eldridge
Dario Fo
Michael Frayn
John Godber
James Graham
David Greig
John Guare
Lauren Gunderson
Peter Handke
David Harrower
Jonathan Harvey
Robert Holman
David Ireland
Sarah Kane

Barrie Keeffe
Jasmine Lee-Jones
Anders Lustgarten
Duncan Macmillan
David Mamet
Patrick Marber
Martin McDonagh
Arthur Miller
Alistair McDowall
Tom Murphy
Phyllis Nagy
Anthony Neilson
Peter Nichols
Ben Okri
Joe Orton
Vinay Patel
Joe Penhall
Luigi Pirandello
Stephen Poliakoff
Lucy Prebble
Peter Quilter
Mark Ravenhill
Philip Ridley
Willy Russell
Jackie Sibblies Drury
Sam Shepard
Martin Sherman
Chris Shinn
Wole Soyinka
Simon Stephens
Kae Tempest
Anne Washburn
Laura Wade
Theatre Workshop
Timberlake Wertenbaker
Roy Williams
Snoo Wilson
Frances Ya-Chu Cowhig
Benjamin Zephaniah

For a complete listing of
Methuen Drama titles, visit:
www.bloomsbury.com/drama

Follow us on Twitter and keep up to date
with our news and publications
@MethuenDrama